POEMOD

(Poem-Of-The-Day)

A Snapshot of Teenagedom In Poems

By Peter Michalski and Andrew Normington

Table of Contents

Welcome to Poemod! We're glad to have you here! As one of the authors of this book, I want to thank you for purchasing, borrowing, pirating, or even stealing this collection of pages. Honestly, I'm just glad you're reading it. However you got here, I want to let you know that you're in for something special. Poemod, as a concept, is a little tricky to grasp without some prior information, so thank you for actually reading the foreword instead of just skipping ahead to the poems. To those who skipped ahead and came back later, you're dead to me. Just kidding. Haha. ANYWAY, let's get started.

Here's how the legend goes.

One January day, in a high school in St. Louis, Missouri, one Andrew "Norm" Normington approached me and told me we should start writing poems. I was confused. We were both already poets, and it seemed strange (and probably impossible?) to start writing poems after we had already started writing poems. But then he continued talking and I apologized for interrupting him mid-sentence after only five words. He explained that we should start writing poems **every day**, and share these poems with one another. As a high school English nerd, I thought this idea was, and I quote, "rad." So for the next seventy-five(ish) days, Norm and I wrote one poem every twenty-four hours, and swapped them whenever we got the chance. This project became Poem-Of-The-Day, or in catchier terms, Poemod.

The Poemod era struck at an interesting time for Norm and me. He was sixteen, I, seventeen, and we were both juniors in high school. For those of you who were never a junior in high school by means of time travel or something, let me catch you up. **Junior year of high school is a weird time to be alive.** It was a time marked by unrelenting schedules, mountains of homework, romantic endeavors, weird social schemas, very little sleep, and everyone's favorite: RAGING HORMONES! But among all the weirdness and stress, we each managed to find real joy, fun, and love mixed in. All the feelings and experiences that we had during this time have been manifested and catalogued and shaken up and splattered over these pages in our daily poems. Some might be great, some might be terrible, but each one of these poems is an authentic and artistic catalogue of some facet of our teenage existences, and I think there's real beauty in that.

I sincerely hope you enjoy reading these poems as much as Norm and I enjoyed writing them.

-Peter Michalski

As the alternate author of this book, I would just like to say that while poems are "rad," they are also very subjective. The truth is juiced from the author and is wearily interpreted by the readers. Especially in regards to mediocre teenage poetry, the meaning can be almost completely unknown by any audience. Quite frankly, I could not remember the motivation of a good 25% of these poems. Regardless, I find that poetry is the perfect outlet for edgy teenagers to vent their struggles. I know what these poems mean to me, but explaining that to you would be impossible.

For the sake of your enjoyment, give your own meaning to my poems. Interpret them in any way you like. If my poem about donuts really speaks to you about capitalism, then feel those feelings you so deeply need to cathart (have a catharsis for) about capitalism. For me, that poem was simply a matter of anger regarding convenience in not dealing with pocket change. These poems mean the world to me because they happened; any other meaning seems irrelevant now. Simply enjoy them and find whatever you need in them to be a better person. Or, if you are just super edgy and you want a reason to be more edgy, that's ok too I guess.

I would like to thank Peter for putting this publishing action together. Although Peter was the subject of exactly zero of my poems, he was genuinely the motivation behind all of them.

Enjoy the read.

-Andrew Normington

I Am Tired

Is it the work I've done

Or the work I haven't?

That plunges me into this muck

This pool of molasses that I've sunken into

Surrounding, and suffocating, and heavy

Swimming up only slows me down, sticks me to myself

Until eventually I'll stop

Stay stuck in sticky solitude

And fall asleep

Peter Michalski

Poemod 1

Donuts!

That shouldn't be much,

But it happened again.

First the soda and the pizza—

Now this?

A donut for a dollar and 5 cents?!

This is insanity.

No more is my wallet of 1$ perfect change—

After this imperfect change.

What's next?

I want to be removed[1] from the school.

There is no God.

Andrew Normington

Poemod 1

---

[1] "Removal from the school" is a polite way for private schools to announce the expulsion of a student.

Webby

Burning across the page, I am master

I fling down numbers, symbols, letters, swift and graceful

Fleeing from the reds of yesteryear towards skies of green

But suddenly I stumble

Fall into a heap among the glyphs

The fuck is a phase constant?

Peter Michalski

Poemod 2

Toasty Disappointment

That buttered toast.

Not to my liking.

No, two fresh buns for me, buttered and broiled.

Slather on some special sauce,

Two maybe three precious tenders—

And a leaf of lettuce.

No lettuce?

E Coli?

Damn.

Andrew Normington

Poemod 2

Day's Daze

It's one of those bizarre days

A contradiction of a square on a calendar

A day you can reach out and taste

You can hear with your own two eyes

And smell with your tongue

A warm stroke in a winter more frigid than most

But with a sun bright enough to match summer's worst

And the sickly fresh wet air that spring blows around

But somehow it feels like fall

Peter Michalski

Poemod 3

Mine Own Dance-Pants Complex

Stop this right now.

That, what you're doing—

What we're doing.

Laughing is good I guess,

But why is it happening now?

It shouldn't happen this way;

Frustratingly it always seems to.

When there are two of you,

Not your usual three.

When there's three there's hardly laughter;

It's so hard to talk to even one.

Yet when there's two—

I'm the third.

She's not there, but I think I feel she should be.

So we laugh at her absence.

I do, anyway.

It's easier, in a sense.

Still I feel the pressure

Weighing on my conscience.

I laugh and forget

Then I leave to try and remember:

Who I am supposed to dance with

And who I want to dance with.

Andrew Normington

Poemod 3

Drought

I'm completely dried up

Like the Sonoran in a drought

Without an idea to quench my withering mind.

I search in the weather, in words, in myself, in others.

But those familiar oases are no longer.

Sopped up by some tormentuous sponge

Some poriferatic poltergeist

Now dripping in a faraway land

As the sand creeps into my ears

And I can no longer hear the splashes that so inspired me

Peter Michalski

Poemod 4

Life Isn't Sung (pt. 1)

Featuring Russell Crowe - "Stars"

The cross you hold so near and dear frowns at the misery you bring its fellow worshipers.

Your marching boots scrape the Paris skyline—

Itching to give scoundrels a kick in the ass.

You understand their ways,

But in your pride you judge them;

In your pride you reign with gargoyles

Joining them as demons of the sky.

Never sharing the force and power,

But instead freezing in the frigid stone that decorates you.

You among the fragile structures of wooden shacks and peasant appetites.

Though it seems your appetite for reward is stronger.

Those that obey are bound to be blessed

And so the poor suffer what they deserve.

You stand there praying that your pursuit of goodness is not deteriorated with the

brutality you Show your Lord's brothers and sisters.

The stars are ordered,

But when you realize the unfathomable disarray—

That lies beyond the sparkling surface,

You remember how your prayers are lost in your own sin.

Now you must do everything you can

To restrain the will from throwing down this Paris skyline,

And with it yourself.

In order to maintain that divine will you have judged on your own.

Then throwing down the stars to maintain the order of God.

Andrew Normington

Poemod 4

Peeping Cur

A little sound peeps in the distance

High and constant and just barely heard

Like an old TV still whirring as it's powered off

The tiny noise beckons me

Just as a cur dog pup whimpers for its cur dog mother

I must be the cur dog mother

I paw towards the sound as it peeps in with greater pour

But the drip begins to drown me

And peeps grow to deafening shrieks

I splash and paddle away as a jet engine flies through my canal

And a thousand cannons flank my other side

And I've yet to meet the whimpers of the peeping cur

Peter Michalski

Poemod 5

When Is a White Cow Not A White Cow

The tender flesh that comforted my lonely soul:

The milkless dugs and eyes of flies,

The lump and imperfections that made me

Love you anyway.

All have been replaced with brittle superficialities.

The splinters taint my hand as I pet you,

And I wonder how it used to be.

You're not there anymore, Milky.

But your soul is engraved in me as I remain comforted

By thee,

Persophone

Andrew Normington

Poemod 5

14

This Poem Will Control Your Mind

"You can now feel the clothes on your body"
A lever is thrown, a switch flips within
And masses of fabric heap upon your skin

"You're now breathing manually"
Inconsistent, inside, a pump pumps and pumps
You're the captain now, your command trumps

"Notice your own blinking"
Lower those shades, those tan, fleshy blinds
And see that I now have a hold of your mind

Peter Michalski

Poemod 6

The Fake One

I nod, not in complacency or understanding.

I crave the connection,

A fake one, at least.

The clock told me I must be tired today.

I don't want to be though.

Just let me be social,

That I may drive home smiling.

Yet there is still more to do.

Music, A pep band

The set up and cleaning

Till I drag myself home

And the clock tells me to be tired again.

Andrew Normington

Poemod 6

Knowledge is Power

How do you know what you need to know

If you don't know what you don't know?

All I know is that I know there's a lot I don't know.

But I don't know how much I don't know

Or when or where or how I'll know what I need to know

Or even what it means to know

Or to not know.

So really, do I know that I know anything?

Or that I don't know anything?

I don't know.

Or do I?

Peter Michalski

Poemod 7

A Good AND Interesting Poem That Breaks All the Rules

I think that big Ol' letters will make it better

No that's two much

No that's too much

Something interesting at least;

So I was sitting there on that squishy soft couch

Everytime I stretched -

Popping joints cracked in the couch's framework-

I stood to investigate

Not all the way.

Just Enough.

But that didn't work, it wasn't enough

So I stayed there in my position and continued my show.

The green characters were walking so fastly

I was very Happy

My legs were not

I sat all the way down and felt the crunch of that squishy soft and fluffy couch

This is a good and interesting day

Today certainly has been

Maybe I will tell this to Joffry, my hamster

And so I wrote it down, ripped it up, and let

Hamster graze on his new, soft and squishy wood chips

Andrew Normington

Poemod 7

White Mountain

Hours of aimless drilling through a white mountain laced with shapes and symbols

On the outside, holes shoot through in clean, straight lines

My fellow prospectors rejoice on the other side

With gold in hand, they tell tales of their skill and strategy

Lost on the inside, I catch echoes of their cries

And try to make sense of the garbled noise

Maybe it'll help me decipher my winding path

I turn circles in the darkness, clinging to the chunk of map I have

Chunks are surprisingly ineffective

The craggy walls croak at me as I tear through the rock

In search of some light, I desperately punch ahead

Finding nothing but rocks, and symbols, and fear, and old paths

As the voices outside mesh and pour into a mocking screech

Reminding me that it's only a matter of time until

A cave-in.

Peter Michalski

Poemod 8

Do You Ever Just

Sit there and think about it for a second?
Contemplating the power in your hands?
Each ritter tatter of keys piling up the story—
To drive their minds wild thinking.
Thinking of importance
Thinking of things that waste time
(better to have not thought of at all)
You could drive the world crazy
You could let them fall in love
You could be the god to the only thing in the world they care about
You could kill those they loved
You could bring them back to life
All because they love that ritter tatter
Piling up the cash
Piling up the emotion that readers never dare let go
Do not fear the power that you have
Just remember the responsibility
You have to pay bills too, ya know
And they have to read books too, ya know
So let them buy and let them cry because you got bored:
Writing that character's life away was so easy for you.
Play God, Play god, play writer, play keys
But next time you feel so inclined
Just write something and make us smile
For no damn reason at all.

Andrew Normington

Poemod 8

Parasitic

A little worm slithers around every person

Manifesting its destiny on face, stomach, mind, and wrist

It cries symbiosis

Boldly claiming its helpfulness to hypnotized ears

But its true intent lies in ravenous greed

Oh how it drains the stomach to a ghostly bowl

Pokes and prods the face into pale stiffness

Berates the mind until it turns on itself

And opens the wrists

Now barren of the life that once was

This little worm lies in each person

Relying on its fat, juicy counterparts and their skeletal hosts

To drive us to feed its cavernous hunger

This little worm conquers each person

Its name?

You already know.

Peter Michalski

Poemod 9

Catching Sushi Burritos

Those massive rolls taunt me,

The fool I am flounders at the thought of them.

This is no role of nature,

But something far beyond me.

Do I seek the rolls or the people?

The people with whom I intend to eat them.

Or rather their roles in my life.

Seeking to dine and laugh with peculiar burritos,

Stuffed with rice and fish

Made larger by societies innovation

Come to me,

Oh sweet pea

Oh golden honey

Oh cream cheese, crab

That I may finally grasp what I have longed

Those rolls of that fish in the sea

At that dining market where I will catch you finally.

Andrew Normington

Poemod 9

Reloj

A white clock meanders along lazily

The grip of time loosens

And the hands seem to slow to a lackadaisical lurch

A minute in five, five in an hour, an hour a day

They decay and crumble

To but a pile of dust in the dirtied rim

Until the clock jumps from the wall

Falls from its place of whiteness

And shatters into a lack thereof

Peter Michalski

Poemod 10

Cards Against Poetry

There is no limit to the mortal

Playing with their precious book

Flipping cards

Their parents too

None can condemn

This sacred game

As long as we keep playing together

Fighting the moral barriers

With peaceful decisions to pretend there's no morality at all

Andrew Normington

Poemod 10

Who?

You lead quite a life when you can't lead in life

Shoot for the wheel but end up shotgun

Your keys are in the hands of another

He looks like you, talks like you, even smells like you

But he isn't you

At least not yet

And maybe that's where you're going

Burning down a highway with no choice but to sit

And listen to music ever too similar to yours

But it's his

Because he's not you

And it's your car

Not his.

So you yank the wheel

And see who's who

Peter Michalski

Poemod 11

It Better Be Me

Fuck, Am I crazy?
I better be crazy
I better be sleep deprived or crazy or something else
I was so happy then and now I have forgotten that
Those precious moments where we were together
And now I question all of that only a day later
Still here with you, but things aren't the same
It better be my mind
My fucking mind that drives itself through the shadow of death flirting with any vile
thought that comes to pass
And so I forget my God and my lovely
My lovely My lovely
She's is my God now
And so I'm trapped in the shadow of death searching for life
Life without hope or God or My sweet lovely
How can my lovely be without you
I tear my mind up on paper to explicate the pain
The frustration
But maybe I'm tired
Dear God let me be crazy
Let anything I have be taken away so I can be happy
Just don't let it be me
Don't let it be me
I hope it's just me
If it's real then my lovely is gone forever
But she's still here
There's still time

Andrew Normington

Poemod 11

Tale of the In-Between

In the fraction of a blink between life and what's next

There's nothing but everything that does and doesn't exist

The tears of flesh swirl up in thick syrupy colors

Pillars of bright blue flame scuffle with orange tsunamis

Crashing together in more of a dance than a fight

Whales take their place in the trees with something not quite like them

And the somethings sing songs but no one is in tune

Yet the sounds blend together with the fire in the waves

Producing a harmonious dissonance that shakes you

You slowly drop to your knees and sink into the purplish mud

Gazing up to the milky green sky, strangely and uncomfortably cool

Until the fraction of a blink ends

And it's on to the next thing

Peter Michalski

Poemod 12

Milk Man

They do not understand who I am
I bring them milk and they tip me—
Poorly I might add
Though I continue to nourish their family

If I wanted to be understood maybe they would know
Those dark nights I spend alone with my cows
Teaching them the routes I take
Where I bring their Milk

It's not mine to give,
But I understand that
They understand that
So do the cows

The cows groan in tender frustration
Leaking away their life
For their young
For my wallet

I nod to the neighbors
They take that thickest Milk
To feed the young and old
Precious and Pure
The Milk that I stole

Andrew Normington

Poemod 12

God I Hate Coffee

The nectar of life flows through me

Swimming and coursing through my stale blood

In caramel copper streams to color my skin and pull me up by the ankles

It lightens my body and alights my eyes

And I feel the coming of the sixth day

But light is followed by darkness

And soon life comes to things better left dead

Drops of red dilute the surging copper

Until its fury bleeds out the brownish dregs

Pulsing, writhing, and threatening to burst through

But coming just short and leaving me scared

Scared that I'll spring a leak

And devolve into a mass of blood and caramel flavoring

Peter Michalski

Poemod 13

The Light

There is no reflection without the light
A divine beauty has been revealed to me
Those heated desires ignite only humility within me
The reflection walks with me and I with she—
Hunger and frigid air tear away at me,
But the light holds my attention.
Giggles fill the air— flowing loosely, constantly—
Raining tremendous emotion like a veil
And now I see differently.
Now I know, though not for sure
The frozen ground like concrete
Echoes a choir of reality.
"Could I kiss you?," I wade in this precious eternity
Content and forgetful, "Once again please..."
Now I bow as a servant begging for more
More humility, more passion and grace
Wanting desperately to remain
I'll keep coming back
I know I won't be the one to stop.
Returning back to fruitful unity
Staring at the reflection of my God
Those youthful blushes warm my soul
Let me stay here please
Face to face with the light
Though you and I know; you have to get home
And I must bring you there

Andrew Normington

Poemod 13

Zero-th Midnight

No midnights gone!

Time jumps into bed, hoping for a story soon

And soon a story there will be

A story of a bunch of in-betweens of child and adult

Throwing it all into a tale they've lived a thousand times before

Time itself waits in agony for the dark to set in

For the pages to flip

For the in-betweens to move and shift

And turn like the wheels of a carriage

Until finally

"Once Upon a Time"

Peter Michalski

Poemod 14

Three

Blotted out reality flows into my view

Recognized only as tests and numbers

Everything I don't know

Otherwise I stare blankly

Filing through those simple items

That hold my full attention:

Those numbers, how I hate them,

The constant labs and questions

The Intense thinking I have no space for:

The girl, yes the girl

I always think of her, never with any room

To think of how to get her.

And the sleep

If I had it I could file through more

Thinking vividly of seven subjects and co-curriculars

But that's ok

The girl's enough

Also I hate science

That's why I write.

Andrew Normington

Poemod 14

The Ballad of S&S

Overfried and underpriced

Teenage life grows here like a spore, creeping and spreading

It's thriving long after midnights past and future

And loud revelries fueled by ice cream and fryer grease

Shake the coop with happy, clucking, feeding

Whipped cream flows through the door,

Flooding out the clucking teens

And leading them home in happy fry-comas

Peter Michalski

Poemod 15

United Provisions Untouched

The silky soda is loaded in the passenger seat

Only an hour there and back

Is there time?

The milk will nourish the fading relationship

Reviving that midnight

A valentine to remind

If only there was time

An hour is plenty for the purchase

But I need more time to think

And so I lose that precious opportunity

And the milk spoils in my passenger seat

As the memory is spoiled in my mind

Andrew Normington

Poemod 15

Satan is From Alaska

I made a deal
Shook hands with a cow
And now the dairy is going to flow

Batter and butter and frozen cream
All mixing together to exact blissful wrath upon my innards
I anticipate the pain, the pleasure, everything

And I wait patiently to consume as I'm consumed

Peter Michalski
Poemod 16

Korea Does it Again

It's soda milk!

It's like a blueberry Go-Gurt

But it's not blueberry

Or a Go-Gurt

And it's soda

It's like those vanilla Tootsie Rolls no one ever eats

But people drink this

And it's no tootsie

Also it's soda

So give it a try

Add some Korean zest to your life

Drink the sodi

Join the cult

Andrew Normington

Poemod 16

Railyard

Adjacent railyards occupy my left peripheral

Boasting a certain beauty

Tugging on time's grasp

Lugging cars just behind the beat

Following some nonexistent drummer

The beast of coal and steel explodes;

Splashes of color burn away the rust

As underappreciated artists flee time, life, and death

Clawing their ways to the left peripheral

And clambering upon the monsters

To tattoo their sufferings onto an apathetic mass

Until it stops trying to stop moving

Submits to time's grasp

And pulls out of the railyard

Peter Michalski
Poemod 17

Stork

That tender flesh so daunting—

So vulnerable—

Regardless of color, that precious package

So beautiful and in need of care

And those eyes:

Unchanging from birth to death bed

With each passing year

Serving as a beacon

Begging each passerby to handle with care

So that fragile and brittle interior remain intact

And those broken pieces like glass won't rip through

That tender flesh

Slicing the hands of the user

Writhing around in Agony

Ruining that precious life

That stork did deliver

Andrew Normington

Poemod 17

No One Is Alone

A kind of happy sadness sprinkles the air around me

A loss not lost but rather gained

An end to a joy that once was

But not a terrible, sad, unhappy ending

A satisfying, beautiful ending

But an ending nonetheless

And I reflect in this sweet salty air as it gets caught in my eyes and mouth

We were what once was but aren't anymore

It's okay because we were and we aren't meant to be always

But in a way we always will be what we were and aren't anymore

And I am and I am not

And the happysad air floats around me and I'm glad it's here

Because it's letting me be what I was and I'm now not

And that's a good thing

Peter Michalski

Poemod 18

No More

Each passing week you spent thinking and planning

But that's all over now

The well worn scripts erase your memories with the return

The costumes are stored away

The wood, nails, and paint are torn apart—

Leaving no trace

The show is done

Another will come

And with it, new people, new family

Yet as you pack away those precious memories you soon forget

Those beautiful people

Those meaningful moments at diners

Each laugh that echoed outside the world of the play

So it's all gone now

None of us want it this way

But it's over

The tears can dry, the waters soar

I weep to think

How could there be no more?

Andrew Normington

Poemod 18

The Great Jell-O Conspiracy

The universe is nothing but a mass of Jell-O

Every crater and orifice pulses with the goo

Each step elicits ripples that elicit the rest

The universe shakes through it all

Always shaking, never moving, never stopping

Just as we shake

We always shake, we never stop

It's because of the Jell-O

It's in our mouths and in our minds

And it's shaking

Always shaking

Never stopping

Peter Michalski

Poemod 19

41

Sweet Idolatry

Not a word nor kiss nor any naked thing
Bares the eternal fulfillment
The satisfaction of union
That I've craved so deeply
For any piece of joy is turned to ash
Where the flame, removed from its source,
Pitters out in my fuelless landscape
So I forget the source and search for embers
But their heat is smothered by my hands
As a hamster in the grip of a child
So adored that the affection collapses a fragile life
And all that is left is cold powder in scorched hands
Blown into the wind by a laughing God
A God whose wind fuels the source
Is the source
And you return, looking for that eternal fulfillment
Then through the light, the words flow through you
The kisses and many naked things are there
Overwhelming and beautiful
But only a single piece
Never comparing, only delighting
Perfectly beautiful,
Held in the source of love.

Andrew Normington

Poemod 19

Speed

Will it catch you?

Spit in the air only to have it return

And slap you in the face

With the smack of a thousand books dropping on a thousand desks

But will it catch you?

Wobble as you move, in tiny oscillations to each side

In gelatinous fervor, your insides jumble

Into a mush of macaroni madness that can't move like this

But will it catch you!?

Even the smallest pebble threatens your life

Demanding your money, phone, keys, and watch

One after another as you bump over and over

BUT WILL IT CATCH YOU!!?

Beyond ground, you continue

As shards of air embed in your eyeballs

And friction suddenly becomes a comfort

Answer the damn question.

It'd better not.

Peter Michalski

Poemod 20

Sweater Weather

Shivering and cold

My back aches with the unnatural recline of my desk chair

I snuggle the thin layers close to chest

No hood

Never a hood

The windows send chilling thoughts

Drowning my torso

I fall asleep

Dreaming that I might go home and sleep some more

Andrew Normington

Poemod 20

ACT

Cut me, crush me, contort me

Do whatever you need

Just make me fit into this box

This numbered box that I've clawed and killed to be in

And that I can't stand to even think about

This mass of paper and ink that slices my fingers, pours on the lemon juice

Every time I hear its name

It bounces around my head, permeates the airspace

Chokes me with ideas and concepts and numbers

Oh the numbers, how I despise the numbers

It assigns us these numbers, these rankings, placements, prices

And value

I'm some old sweater at a garage sale

Slap a sticker on me, give me the value I so desire

As long as it's enough

Otherwise it's best I be thrown away, left for the dog to tear apart

With the sticker left unwrenchable upon me

A symbol of value in just a number

A number assigned by some machine that can't read anything more

Than soft leaded number 2 pencils

Please fill in the bubbles completely

Peter Michalski

Poemod 21

Dry Hands

The moisture that soaks the ground

The snow that finds its way down my neck

Trickling and warming to water droplets

Will never reach my hands

The crisp breeze drains me

The snowflakes taunt me

As these winter days steal my life from me

And leave me with dry hands

Crackling hands

Where joints break the dead skin

Then tear the fresh meat underneath

Droplets of blood

And so I lose my voice as the wind swarms around me

Crying in a puddle of agony

Where the winter stole my life from me.

Andrew Normington

Poemod 21

The Short One About Avocado Sauce

A cold green mash of mush

To drown your sorrows

In Mexican food that isn't even Mexican

But some American crap

Made of the feet of pigs

Wearing a sombrero

All I can taste is avocado sauce

What the hell is guacamole?

Peter Michalski

Poemod 22

And a Plain Bagel

I just need one thing to get me going

One simple thing with one simple hole

Spread the cheese and toast it please

Perhaps an egg and bacon

All I need is a plain bagel

And some coffee

To make this morning worth it

Andrew Normington

Poemod 22

Something More

Needs a pinch of zizz

Some incandescent sparkly thing
Something to catch the eye
Put it in a jar
And present it as a B range science project

Just a hint of a whisper of some pop
Some symbol of a cymbal in the ear
Some fortissimo timpani whack to scare the audience
And give even Haydn some ninety-four nightmares

An idea of a whiff
Like a kitchen cooked in hours ago
With baked in aromas of clove and rosemary
Hanging lazily in clouds, just barely brushing the nostrils

Or maybe just a drop of zazz

Peter Michalski
Poemod 23

Tumble

(Inspired by the kid who fell out of his chair on stage during Newsies)

With the piercing clamor of my alarm

I tumble out of bed

Because I'm hardly ever there

I tumble through chorus

When I'm behind on my history

I tumble in names and dates

I simply never practice

I tumble through Spanish

The math and science means nothing to me

I tumble and pretend I don't care

I sit in English class

Everything is peaceful

I am sturdy here

Andrew Normington
Poemod 23

Bested!?

Bested again!

By a world that shames the dishonest

And shoves cash into their fists

By a world that pours hot soup on the mind

Driving the youth to militant defense

All for the sake of the arbitrary

This meaningless contest

That boasts nonexistent status

Stolen by the cold voice of some woman in a phone

And given to the unscathed outlaws

Who don't even give a shit

And leave the rest clawing for the nothing that was in their grasp once

It hurts more when the nothing isn't there

Peter Michalski

Poemod 24

Ain't That The Truth

Thanos could be defeated

The Devil, his angels too.

Voldemort and any antagonist written away

With the desire of a morally guided artist.

Even so, with the Bible and Koran alike

With every PSA and conference

With every warning and guideline

With a clear set of simple moral basics

That anyone with eyes and ears could see

All is ignored

And so that undefeated idiocy of fools and cowards

Loiters to ruin the fun of those who try

and those who think

And those who sacrifice for morality

All is sucked up

By dirty, motherfucking cheaters.

Andrew Normington

Poemod 24

Zombie

Fueled by scum and carbohydrates

I lurch through the day in a sort of glazed discomfort

The feeling that there's always something tugging on my right arm

With wrists burned by this rope, I march along to the tune of a single note

This note that opens doors to more doors that close in five minutes

And within those doors I simply wait for the next note

As that rope dries out my skin and itches my knuckles

And the glaze thickens as I stumble lifelessly between the endlessness

They call me a zombie as they feast on my brains

Peter Michalski

Poemod 25

Something Like That

Surely it has to do with clouds and light

Certainly there are streets of gold

It wouldn't be Heaven without my lover

It wouldn't be Heaven without my Lord Jesus

It wouldn't be Heaven without Muhammad

It wouldn't be Heaven without Abraham

Eternal paradise must have all those things I wish for

Or else it wouldn't be paradise

Surely I will find an eternity to watch my favorite shows

To seduce those lovely women

The perfect pleasures of paradise

All that booze and liquor

Those fights, how I love to fight

All the things I could ever want

I want them here, but here's not Heaven

Surely they must be there

Surely Heaven is everything I think it is

Or something like that

Andrew Normington

Poemod 25

Eggs on the Mind

Scramble my brains into yellow goo

Because I need more protein in my diet

Those tiny little LEGO bricks

To build a tower high enough to support my droopy skull

Hard boil that skull and maybe salt it a little

So that yellow ball of flavorless mush stays where it belongs

And the rest stays fresh for a few hours

Or just fry the whole thing

Cover it with greens to make it interesting

Some flavor never tried but always beckoning

Fried might just be the way to go

Peter Michalski

Poemod 26

Jellyfish

Flowing with the current

Everything is fine

There is no need to worry

There are somethings you can't control

So flow with those tides

Pray never to find yourself on shore

Being prodded with a beach stick

By any random passerby

Try never to sting

Only in defense

Everything will be fine

Flow with the current

Live, because you are alive

Andrew Normington

Poemod 26

Lusting For Better Weather

A drop of warm water teases me as I wallow in this bucket of ice

It's the sweat off the shirt of some beautiful woman

Some sultry goddess with a smile that screams of mischievous freedom

And with a body strong enough to break me in two

I'll see her every now and again from my place in this bucket

She'll give me a wink that shines through this glacial nightscape

Or maybe blow me a kiss on some warm breeze

But she never reaches in

Never opens her arms and legs, and probably never will

At least not until this damn ice melts

Peter Michalski

Poemod 27

A Haiku

Who thought all was well?

Is this really worth the time?

Don't forget to live

Andrew Normington

Poemod 27

Trade-Off

Priorities are a finicky thing

They skip between the various burdens

Like a child in a field of daisies

Hundreds of thousands of daisies

Each prettier than the last

Beckoning to the child

As it stumbles along in frantic frenzy between all

Trying to see and smell and pick

Alas, a single child can't handle such a task

And the daisies grow exponentially

Surrounding the child in thick and powerful stalks

And it has nothing but a handful of daisies

Slowly wilting beneath the towering flowers

Peter Michalski

Poemod 28

The Perfect Plan

A movie and dinner seems the way to go

I have pre-written conversations

Unfortunately there isn't a way to know

Where the night could take us.

I hope for laughter and fluidity

I hope the movie's good

I pray we forget about the movie

Walking away, wondering what ever happened to that protagonist

And his friends

Flailing along in oblivion

Understanding where our focus lies.

How does Golden Corral sound for dinner?

Andrew Normington

Poemod 28

The Write Time

A friar once told me, "Night time is the right time."

So as dusk dims the homes of the world

My lamp springs to life

Bathing paper in a rich yellow glow

Dousing my notebook in a fine honey

And I fly

Molding worlds from words in a chaotic cacophony

Rife with order and poise and grace

Puddles of ink coagulate with such great energy

Sticking together with some mystically magnetic attraction

Joining to form letters, words, sentences,

Poems.

Peter Michalski

Poemod 29

Watch Your Step

That tender flesh, so vulnerable,
Conquers every creature
Never succumbing to difficulty
Breaking through rocks
Climbing and cutting each branch
Slicing the earth in two
So it might keep each:
The bigger and the smaller half.

That tender flesh, so daunting,
Standing like a god
Commanding strength through
difficulty
Molding rocks into statues
Chopping branches, making crosses
Feasting at tables
Lounging on thrones
So the workers know who's boss.

That tender flesh, so forgetful,
Teaches every creature
Preaches love through difficulty
Takes every stone for a temple
To leave nothing for the homeless
Forging forests into paper
Writing books and acting against them.

That tender flesh, so lonely,
That precious package, in need of care
Rolling that boulder on a mortal journey
Careful not to stumble.

That tender flesh, so blissful,
Waltzes on the peaks of mountains
Crumbles avalanches on the highways
that took him there
Feasts on the grape vine
Drinks in eternal day
Forgetting the boulder that's supposed
to be with him.

That tender flesh, those eyes,
Unchanging from birth to death bed
Serving as a beacon
Begging each passerby
to handle with care
So that fragile interior remains intact
And those broken pieces — like glass —
won't rip through
Tearing that tender flesh apart.

Andrew Normington

Poemod 29

62

Cows Cry Criminy

"Criminy!" exclaim those sopping sponges

Overfilled cows waiting for sunrise

To unload their burdens

And let someone else handle the milk

Their legs twist and quiver under the weight

Waiting for some farmer to dry them out

Make them frail and brittle

And bake them in warm summery glowering glows

Or for some butcher to slice them open

Take off a few pounds

Achieve that New Year's resolution

Fry up something good to break the others'

But no matter how you slice it

Or milk it

Or dry it, or bake it, or whatever

Just lighten this load

Peter Michalski

Poemod 30

I'm Cold

The slick fingers fumble and slide through the sweat

Wipe them on the jeans and the hands are dry,

Everything is fine

But now the jeans are drenched

The hands are cracked

The winds freeze the droplets

The hands crack and bleed

The pants are cold

The winds swirl and suffocate

There is no warmth

There is no light

No cloth can shield

The pain I feel

My hands are cold.

Where's the morphine?

Andrew Normington

Poemod 30

A Tale of Two Watches

All of existence is kept in balance
By the fact that I wear two watches

Time refuses to bend and break
And dance like a toddler at a birthday party
The leather straps that hug my wrist
Secure that great beast down by its haunches
And reduce its flamboyant, juvenile thrashing
To a steady series of ticks and tocks

But it must be two!
A single watch will follow time's persuasion
Passive and unresisting, it slows its tocks
And falls into time's embrace
But three is too fierce
Three overwhelm the beast, scare it, tie it too tight
Confuse it into a ticking beyond rhythm and reason
Throwing it all into a chaotic cyclone
But two is beautiful
Two watches waltz in perfect time
To the beat of tocks and ticks from their tamed pet
They complement each other
Keep the other honest and keep the animal in check
Balancing all of existence

Peter Michalski

Poemod 31

I'm Confused

These stairs are dry

At least they appear to be

Still I slip and slide

Blind to the ice that so wets my knees

As I fall to the bottom.

I climbed so far

But the steps deceived me

I will find dry clothes

And eat a wholesome meal

Somewhere else

Where the doors are open

Andrew Normington

Poemod 31

Gates

Scramble way way down

To the gates of Hell for warmth

Or maybe a chat

Or jump way way up

Try to dive between the pearlies

Look cool doing it

Or stay where you are

Smell the soil beneath you

Save gates for later

Peter Michalski

Poemod 32

Patience

The silly boy sits and waits

He's not stupid

His mother is gone.

Forever perhaps.

But maybe he'll wait just a bit longer

Lingering on a bench of suffering

Until he hears the dirt tumble down

Filling the void

But the dirt never comes

And the boy never leaves

He just sits there

Wondering

Suffering

Where could his mother be?

Andrew Normington

Poemod 32

Knee

With a crack like lightning

And a smack like thunder

Your bad decisions knee you in the face

And your teeth fall right out

And your nose turns bright red

And your jaw gets fucking blasted to space

So you see, as you're hit

That you've missed quite a bit

And you crumple to the floor in disgrace

Peter Michalski

Poemod 33

And So it Ends

I guess I'm crazy.

I sit there in the audience

Listening to my god

Begging forgiveness from my God

For that Idolatry

I have worshiped you

In plans and dreams

You were my goal

You were my purpose.

Now I burn in this Hell

As you smile at me—

No, the conductor.

But it sure looks like it

And you sing no siren's hymn

Nor precious melody.

You sing *And So it Goes*

A glorious torture to tear at my soul.

The song mocks me and you smile.

For in every heart there is a room

Mine was one of planning.

A heart of logic.

Where I knew with every move

I loved you

And I thought you loved me too

For I gave you my heart to break

And I feared what I said so I sat in
silence

And maybe you forgot me

If you had any memories at all

Maybe that was my worst mistake

And so I sit in hell with that mistake

And so it goes

And so it went

And so it ends, today

There is nothing else

The hope is lost in that room

Ablaze with my planning

Every memory a self deceit

Please Lord, end the song.

End my suffering

Andrew Normington

Poemod 33

Both Ends Dripping

The room burns brightest if you light both ends.

Wax drips in puddles, first moist

Then frozen indefinitely

Until someone scrapes it up into a million useless flakes

I can't let myself be scraped up

Let me retain my puddley essence

So please, oh God please, keep the cold winds away

Peter Michalski

Poemod 34

Jump!

People's eyes don't jump

They stay plain and simple

Always running away together

The muscles won't allow any other way.

When they look at others

There is no muscle

And any glance might turn away the locked stare

Leaving each other entirely at the mercy

Of those harsh winds that seduce moisture—

Now those eyes are drained.

Always turning and looking together

For another pair to lock in security

Still always they look away

Until those muscles connect

And they have no choice to look away

For in that infinity they look and praise

Until those muscles stun themselves in pleasure

Now they look away

If they don't look back

What pain will be?

Those muscles are all we have

To lock ourselves in Eternity.

Andrew Normington

Poemod 34

At Trek's End

Stardates buzz by with a whirr and a flash

And the captain's log just can't keep up

Because the sun eats itself up

Starving for a hint of something familiar

It chows down on the inside

Shrinking like some baseball

Slammed into a home run but never reaching home

And mankind's great and peaceful Enterprise

Blasts into a breakneck orbit

And shatters another mach with each turn

Endlessly flushing into such great brilliance

That then yields to nothingness

Peter Michalski

Poemod 35

To Be Real

It hurts to think of it
Really it does.
And I know now
It hurts when you're real.
No meaningless distraction can truly outweigh
My affection for you.
Those moments we shared
They were real.
More than just a fantasy
You are no object
To be flushed from my memory.
Let me be real
Let me show my love for you.
I have every reason to be dissatisfied
You still reign in your seeming perfection
A child of God
I knew that
Truth does not change
And so my soul disdains to think
Of how it could have ended differently.
It hurts now
Because it was real
Because you are still real
Thank God
That I am real.

Andrew Normington

Poemod 35

Chords of Cord

Untwist, untie, unravel
Go the thinnest cords
The sharpest silk from the fattest worms
The webs that mark the dusty corners

The grand piano falls out of tune
Shouting only dissonant patterns
Dreaming of the chords of old
And the wood rots
Decay eats it up like locusts at a harvest festival
Ripping apart any beauty that once was

Eventually the thinnest thin so thin
That each side whips away
As lovers, burned by their scalding passions
And silence envelops the cracked keys

Peter Michalski
Poemod 36

The Perfect Lie

The Brain pulses in unrealistic designs

The child colors outside the lines

If only they were better.

There's always something more

Never settle for less

You can grab life by the reigns

And gallop into the sunset

Riding with your trophy, *Perfection*.

They never told you, though.

How wild that horse can be

No spur nor rope can contain

The brutal rearing

Where riders fly, like loose cargo

Flailing onto the ground.

But they never call for help.

What would they think?

If they came and saw you

Covered in dirt and dust.

Yet it was there where you saw the light.

So you walk in bare feet

Now watch the horse run—

You never had any control

Just observe the natural beauty.

Now comfort the child,

And color outside with him.

Andrew Normington

Poemod 36

Poetic Rebellion

Words will and work and bend and warp themselves
To fit a certain box with certain name
To stack and sort and rot away on shelves
And only their creators are to blame
Revere these formats! Worship them as gods!
Say the salty ones, always turning back
With a bloodlust for weirds, stranges, and odds
And beady gazes, murd'rous eyes turned black
But the deep disdain forces me to ask
To wonder, dream, or even wish about
Some dastardly, devilish, daring task
To steal from them what they can't live without
Perhaps my plunder is the final line.

Peter Michalski
Poemod 37

Towels

Here they are

Thrown into a pile

For those feeble men

Fully aware of the forces

They have fallen to

Faking their efforts

No sweat to dry

Evolution has done no good

Give them their crutches

Wrap the towels on their head

So they go blind to reality

They cannot lose

What they do not have

Andrew Normington

Poemod 37

To Wind

Slice the sky in bold and careful strokes

Rumble and tangle with the stars themselves

Scream for those you've lost and miss so dearly

Course through the world and let us feel your pain

Though please spare *us* from such great tantrums and griefs

We desire not to feel your sorrows

We'll feign empathy but we won't shed a tear

And you'll get nothing if houses collapse

We ask you to cease your blust'ry passions

To cancel your wails and woes and whimpers

We really can't take your constant barrage

And the world simply will not understand

Scream and slice and rumble beyond us

Express your feelings, just do it elsewhere

Peter Michalski

Poemod 38

The Signs

The grumbling master spits on the boy.
The innocent are blind to truth.
There is nothing but disappointment;
As far as he's concerned.

Synched sandals and clean robes:
Those are not enough for him.
The boy must see clearly
Every miracle before his eyes

Still the boy looks beyond for deeper
meaning
Failing still to see the truth
And the master shakes his head
Look at what I'm showing you

Now the boy runs to his mother
Weeping at the abuses
And he remains blind
To all the miracles before him.

The next day, the master stops
And the boy fends for himself
There is nothing to see
But the boy keeps looking

The master acts his miracles again
Out of pity and reconciliation
In desperation the boy cries aloud
What am I looking for?

The master works harder
Trying to make the boy see
I have given you everything!
The boy is angry now

Telltales swarm the boy,
And he tells the master what he sees.
It's wrong, it's wrong
You son of a bitch

The boy strikes his master down
A temper tantrum to end the pain
All I wanted was to understand
But the master is dead

Now there is nothing left
The boy is suffocated in isolation
Cry boy, Cry: You've failed,
There are no more signs. It's all your
fault.

Andrew Normington

Poemod 38

80

Reunion

It's been far too long since we last encountered

You're a completely new experience

And I still can't remember who you once were

But that doesn't matter to you and I

Because we

are.

And that's what matters.

Peter Michalski

Poemod 39

The Loser's Club

Happy Birthday!

And welcome to your initiation.

We see that you're already crying,

But don't panic

Soon enough you'll stop; we all do.

You depend on us to survive

But we rely on you for hope

It's really an uphill battle

Still though, we try.

You will look for an escape,

I'm afraid there is none.

No money or fame

Will redeem you from humanity.

The kings lose mothers

The presidents, their fathers

And Darling too,

you'll find that you lose

Not only your love, but your mind.

So welcome to The Loser's Club!

We'll mock and spit

Feel free to join us

There's no need to accept one another.

Forever in The Loser's Club—

This home we call earth

Paradise provides:

there's always something to lose

If only, Darling, we could choose.

Andrew Normington

Poemod 39

Weak Week

A barrage of cannonfire explodes on my back

I fire back, but to no avail

My efforts are for naught

Hours upon hours of digging these trenches

Powdering the cannons, lighting the fuses

But a well placed shell undoes my doings

Desertion is all that's left for me

Sweden beckons with a sultry pull of the finger

Alas, I didn't jump in time

Peter Michalski

Poemod 40

Something New (A Haiku)

Time for a new plan

She's not a good idea

Where will I go now

Andrew Normington

Poemod 40

The Exam Haiku

Sapped of energy

My will to make destroyed by

Physics party tricks

Peter Michalski

Poemod 41

I'm Forgetting This After the Test (A Haiku)

Words and words and words

A dog can only learn some tricks

Don't forget to sleep

Andrew Normington

Poemod 41

Life, The Universe, and Everything

A crumb on the floor is nothing like a black hole
One conquers entire galaxies with dispassionate wrath
The other lies complacent, ignoring its own existence

But they are the same thing.

Floating through the cosmos lurks some equation
Some combination of nothingness
Strolling some starstream
Unaware of its importance
And its power, terrifying and awesome

Its is the tree of knowledge we dearly paid for
And it embodies the why, how, when, where, who, what
Links the crumb to the black hole with no second thought
And questions the validity of chickens and eggs
All in utter oblivion
Huddled away in some pocket in some nook in the universe

It offers no answers
Only the question.

Peter Michalski

Poemod 42

How Hard

Where is that perfect stance?
The one where the mind
rests in equilibrium
A place of tranquility and diligence
So that no work can disgrace
An easy going mind.
How much sleep is too little?
When you shouldn't be driving
But that paper's due
And no one gives a shit anyway.
Can we draw the line?
Or at least provide expectations
Instead of this relative chaos
Where hard workers try to keep up
And the lazy ones lie as they must
So that society still stands.
Do not say to me,

"You're not working hard enough"
I assure you, I know what I'm doing
For fuck's sake we work
till we're not human
And there seems to be no inbetween
Or else you fall to the social darwinism
No one cared about you anyway
No one in the real world cares anyway
So work like a dog
Because that's what you really are
Your emotions mean nothing
Everyone cares
Until no one cares
And you're stranded on the street corner
Desperate for some work.

Andrew Normington
Poemod 42

88

Good Empty

I've completely emptied myself

Every word on a page

Every argument filed away

And I'm now empty

Not a sad, cold empty

A different empty

An emptiness knowing

That there's room within

Peter Michalski

Poemod 43

Nonsense

Blee Blee screeb deeb

Shmorble dorbling son of a gun

Hobling blee screeb

On that precious flower

Scallipanopsis to blonder donder

Scliperdipper shmulmber

Dingle dandle dimby boy

Bottled bambie bumble

Bringet, brondledondle

Skiddle dee dee

Do not look into thee

Andrew Normington

Poemod 43

Scroll

Scroll

Scroll

Scroll

Rub my thumb against the glass

Until it burns off

And I'll post about the ashes

Peter Michalski

Poemod 44

Everything's Fine

That shimmering gold

Made me a fool

When I bit into its core

And found nothing

Nothing but confusion and concern.

Still that gold is pretty

And the shell maintains

That youthful luster

Which lured me in

To take a bite

Where the apple seed core

Leaked cyanide into my veins

And now I see nothing

When I used to see everything

Glowing clearly in the light

Of that fool's gold

Andrew Normington

Poemod 44

Strawberry

Cold and strikingly red

Like a freckled face on a January afternoon

The speckled something takes its place among the others

Starring, writing, and directing its own great show

Leading the cast with a green crown and a tart bite

Earning rave reviews across the nation

And blushing hard at the final bows

Peter Michalski

Poemod 45

Don't Look Too Closely

Doesn't it look like

Things were meant to go wrong

The fruit was eaten

And centuries of tainted blood

Cycled through and cities burned.

Now the perfection cannot be reached

And it's all ok that way

When you don't stare too long

Lingering at the bumps and bruises

Where the failures took their toll.

So long as you get lost

Wandering in the beauty of it all

Forgetting those mistake

And hardships

To see the beauty off the bigger picture

The way it was meant to be seen

Andrew Normington

Poemod 45

Dry Shoulders, Wet Eyes

The sight of another's pain

Exposed to my virgin eyes

My shoulders were dry and cracked before

But sudden rain storms explode with the flashiest floods

And the dams crumble away

My shoulders are grateful for the quenching

But let's hope no one gets hurt

Peter Michalski

Poemod 46

If You Knew

If only I knew what I wanted

Then I would stop wasting my time

Banging on this glass door

Begging to come inside.

It's warm in that mansion—

At least I think it's a mansion,

I've only ever seen the door.

I only think it's warm, too.

How could I ever be sure.

I've never been inside

This precious palace I have made.

All I see is you lounging

In the living room

By the fireplace

Where I see that warmth

That home of mine

In my mind.

So I bang on the door

Please let me in

And that glass shatters

Stricken with reality

And I feel no warmth.

Still though you sit there.

While the fire burns out

And I know I must leave

This shack of my own demise

You bring me no warmth

Except where that fire died

Burning within my mind

Andrew Normington

Poemod 46

Avian Flight Patrol

Sparrows soar downwards

In great and wonderful and tight bombing patterns

Perfect for the Saturday Evening Post

They flee hands pale and clammy

Flailing wildly, pushing air in all directions

Violently grasping as prey dodge and dive

Towards another set of arms

Supple

Healthy

Darker

The arms accept the sparrow fleet

In a close and cozy protection

From the clutches of winters past

Peter Michalski

Poemod 47

Boredom

Where is the peace of mind

That comes from absolutely nothing

Why does the nothingness

Do something to my brain

Where nothing entertains

And no desire can ignite

A passion within me

To write or eat or think

Or practice or play

Rather I stare at nothing

So that one day

I might be happy

Doing something again

Andrew Normington

Poemod 47

Elegy of Allergy

RED ALERT!

Skies crack, shatter, and fall

The air around you goes cold and stagnant

It flees your body through every pathway

Leaves you empty and dim and dusty inside

Just as a soul might escape a fresh corpse

And everything suddenly goes bright red

Red and itchy

A swarm of fire ants surrounding you

Feasting on your flesh like it's fast-fired pizza

The rosy virus nests in the eyes

Opens the great big floodgates

And wets the whole damn face

There you lie, now

A zombie, a husk of what you once were

Because spring has sprung

A surprise attack

Peter Michalski

Poemod 48

Thunderstruck

When God came down,

I did not quite believe

What I was believing

Until a year of convincing

Told myself that the beauty was real

So I could truly open my eyes

And confirm its reality.

So I stared and touched

And twice I checked

And twice confirmed

The clouds were dark

Still the lightning flared so vibrantly

Now pinch me in this dream.

So that I open my eyes

For what I was told to glorify

Was simply just a dream

Even though I feel the burn

Of that lightning

And I stare baffled

Praying for those thunder clouds.

But their rain is done

The dream is over.

Now I'm left with nothing to glorify

And I weep at the clouds

I'm not sure were ever there.

Andrew Normington

Poemod 48

100

Rhymes With Space

Way up there

Where ice is air

And planets make their home

Black holes sigh

And comets fly

And astronauts, they roam

Darkness lurks

Starlight is shirked

In nothing's vast biome

Peter Michalski

Poemod 49

Come to the Fair!

The fair was full of delight

Until raggedy ann

Got too close.

The fair was full of fright

As the tents collapsed

In balls of fire

And the cotton candy burned so bright

Torching the petting zoo

Lambs ran in painful silence

The fryers gave heart attacks

To the panicking crowds

The grease and starch

Sucked their life away

And they fell to the fires

Consuming their loved ones

Their families.

How fun the fair looked

Now they burn

And those kids at the top

Screaming on the ferris wheel

Count the seconds

Before the ride lowers them to flame.

Who started this fire?

When will it stop burning

When will it end

Will there ever be laughter again?

Andrew Normington
Poemod 49

102

Poemod Fifty

Goodness, gosh, and golly we've been through gobs

Of poems great and small and in between

Despite the gobs, we'll keep writing these songs

These sweet etudes of pain and love and hope

And the occasional really weird one

A hardcore rap track played on a banjo

To relate the world to gelatinous ooze

They continue past any expiry

The record's diameter never ends

Emotions, observations persevere

In letters, words, lines, verses, and stanzas

In notebook pages dripping black with ink

And in a mass of code and bright pixels

Thundering loud in some great unseen cloud

Peter Michalski

Poemod 50

It's Time

What are you supposed to do

When you have no control

And all you can do is wallow

Rolling in a pool of self pity.

The time will not align again

It aligned once, and that was enough

The universe began

And time will never align again.

What we have is permanent

Our past and future too.

It will happen whether we like it or not

There's nothing we're supposed to do.

You could try not to think

How you're born a year off

Or how the train left without you

But don't do that.

There is time for you.

Come and see the time you have

Things will align

Though not quite in rhyme

With the world around you.

Maybe you'll stumble and fall

Right where you should be—

Meeting time face to face

Now fall forever

Fall in love

Until time stops ticking for everyone

Andrew Normington

Poemod 50

Morning Person

Shut off the lights

Let me bake in a blue glow

And eat Cheetos until I burst

Morning sings its silent songs

The rest of the world ignores

But from my desk I hear the siren's calls

She crescendos with the sun

Gracing the ears of the rest of the world

And I slip away to the sound

Peter Michalski

Poemod 51

Fresh Slippers

I will not put them on,

These furry shoes.

They look so cozy,

But I simply cannot afford:

The extra pounds,

The lying around,

The shuffling sounds

When I must move on—

Dragging the slippers with me

As they resist the pull

And I must slip out

To live my day in full.

Perhaps I'll try the tennis shoe.

Those do not fall off.

I would be locked in—

Ready to jog and run

Oblivious to the outside world.

And I would be healthy.

Still, though,

My feet would get tired and sore.

So when I'm lost and weary

And the work is done.

I can settle down

To slip on those furry shoes

No shuffling sounds

No dragging on.

I can be content then,

Loving the rest of my day

As I give myself fully

To those fresh slippers of mine.

Andrew Normington

Poemod 51

What Isn't There

Why fear the dark?

In an absence of light

The absence doesn't strike us

Possibility bares its fangs

What might be sharpens its claws

And we run screaming from the horrible beasts

But they follow not far behind

Pick up a scent and make a new home

Push darkness into the mind

So they have room to run and jump

And rattle the whole body

With the fear they whisper through

Peter Michalski

Poemod 52

Don't Make Me Come Down There

While I sat upon my planning stool

I drew up masterpieces

To play the fool

The fool I was

And the fools around me.

I'd play them all,

Complete in foundry.

So "Perfect!" I'll say

And God surely will laugh

So mightily he might sway

Right off of his throne

And topple on down

Back to earth

Then slap the fool

That brought him back so soon.

But such things happen

To those damn men

Who forget God

In their perfect plan.

Andrew Normington

Peomod 52

Absorbent Morning

Little flecks of light dot the horizon
Arranged by some dispassionate sweep
Like bits of eraser on an imperfect canvas

Pinpricks punch the blues through
And let bits of white drip down
Pooling into some milky substance
That seeps into the earth's veins and arteries
Sweeps the landscape too
Keeping it all fresh

Peter Michalski
Poemod 53

Ambitions

Conquer and be feared

No one shall stand

Except those you lead.

Let no one have mercy

Slice them to bits

With every decision

That benefits the *you*.

And stand strong now.

Another is coming

Who will shred your aspirations

And throw you to the dogs

Where your ideas rot

And your mind is nothing

Anymore

Andrew Normington

Poemod 53

Inspiration in Three

A waltz in an empty ballroom

With a woman out of thin air

Who gracefully glides around you

Moving in unrestrained, glorious passion

While still keeping time to the strings

You reach out, desire possessed

Longing for nothing but to match her

To further her beautiful intensities

And complete them

To shake the very planet with such an outpour of greatness

Alas, the song comes to a close

She returns to earth, her trance complete

Puts a hand to your cheek, smiling

And fades into the oxygen that fills your head

Maybe next time

Peter Michalski

Poemod 54

Coca Cola

The cane sugar drips

Lingering on glass bottles

Flying from cans.

Days of work

Hours on buses

Hold me from

Your precious sustenances.

Oh New York

Big Apple

Small apples

It's all the same to me.

So long as I don't grapple

Too long

Just give me that drink

Like cocaine for a druggie

That special glass

Of pure Coca Cola

Andrew Normington

Poemod 54

Screen Burn

I look into my phone and step within

To see universes melt and blend together

Masses of text and code crash against each other

Like waves on an angry ocean

And my eyes grow wearier every minute

Peter Michalski

Poemod 55

Room 44

It's a bit too crowded

These unexpected visitors

In this Room 44

This Room 4 4

This Room Four 4

In this Room For 4

I can take no more.

Stop the emails.

Andrew Normington

Poemod 55

Tomorrow

Tomorrow always finds me

Where I'm not today

In places and people and faces

Travel and touch and feel the feelings

Of unfelt feels

That tomorrow thrusts upon me

Peter Michalski

Poemod 56

The Ought To Be

Lovers' eyes don't jump
They linger easily— willfully.
Only running away together
To the next heated moment
Where locked eyes seduce eternity
Over and over again.
There the minds learned everything,
There ideas became idea
And that only idea is love.
So through every mess and struggle
The unity that was conceived
Pulls those lovers back again.
And with these cycles grows certainty
That matrimony is the only option.
So lovers surrender themselves
Truly— fully.
Where their love is committed as idea
Until their love becomes life
With breaths of reality.
There is no time to sleep,
only to nurture.
Their life has changed.

But when breath forgets
from where it came
Parents chide themselves
for teaching independence.
The lovers are left alone.
Broken hearted, blind to the past
Till unity pulls them back again
For no mind, no matter how tormented,
Could break from itself
Except in death.
Ultimately then, death—
That mighty fault
in the human condition—
Jolts apart that welded union
And the lover loses half of
who they were.
Content still, the broken one knows
Their love was as full
as it could have been.

Andrew Normington

Poemod 56

The Return

I've been floating for a while

On my back, upside down,

Barreling through the oddities of space

Shooting past stars and moons and the like

Entire civilizations, existences, timelines

Are but a blur in my fast moving eye

And so I wonder what propels me

What draws me in

Tugs on my invisible strings

Begins my journey and keeps the fuel coming

Until it reveals itself

The puppet master

A star of blinding and dazzling beauty

No longer pulling, but beckoning

And I accept its calls

Peter Michalski

Poemod 57

How Dare

When you have walked away from everything

And that light shines in the darkness

You see that everything is illuminated

Now that you are no longer smothering it.

You loaded the fire with leaves

With no right to destroy

Such green shrubbery.

Stand from a distance now

Watch as the caretakers

Revive what you wounded.

How dare you take control

That fire was never yours to burn.

Andrew Normington

Poemod 57

Saw It Coming

Congratulations, you've claimed another

Another soul, optimistic and bright

Who saw a future through his glasses

He had promise, so you did what you had to

Beat him, surrounded him, kicked him on the ground

Cut out his tongue, but slowly, piece by piece

Boiled him alive and watched him shrivel

And stomped him out when he fought back

Peter Michalski

Poemod 58

Free Him

How do you blame him

The child, the boy

Who did nothing but work

To please everyone

While no one cared.

What good is life

Obsessed with misery

As the mind tortures itself

Starved for perfection.

There is fault to be placed

On nothing and no one.

Not even the boy.

Help him

Stop hiding from his pain.

You bastards claim to know everything

But you Know nothing

Deceived from common anxieties.

Free him

Before that chair is knocked away.

And he hangs there

Freed from his torturous reality.

Andrew Normington

Poemod 58

DnD

A prick of a prince might be your escape

Or perhaps some goliath, towering in stupidity

Or an elf, an orc, a werewolf, whatever

Just stuff yourself with pizza

And go along for the ride

Gamble such valuable hit points

On the cold judgement of a 20-sided die

Surrounded by the lives that depend on it

Watch your odds float for a split second

And get killed by a monster

Peter Michalski

Poemod 59

PhotoShop

Welcome to the Photo-Shop!

It's dangerous here,

But bear with me.

As deceit leads you to enjoyment

And everything is perfect.

Where ladies are lovely

And each man has no mole.

Everything you dream

Is in this illusion.

Stand here forever

Locked in lies and torture

This is what you want.

To believe what you see

In hopes that it might be real.

Andrew Normington

Poemod 59

Eck

That day of

Reckoning beckons

Checks and inspects

My chest and neck

Elects to inject

Itself into my texts

It expects some regret

To mend and correct

Intending to bend

Each fleck, to wreck

Each tiny speck

Until it reflects for a second

Peter Michalski

Poemod 60

Gold

If you know what you want,

Then you go and you find it.

And you take it.

Do not fiddle around

With the in between

Give your conscience no room

No time to think.

Act on the impulse

Grab that lamp

And rub the crap out of it.

So you may have your wish

Only to be fooled

By your mind.

You never grabbed the lamp,

You didn't have the guts.

Andrew Normington

Poemod 60

A Messy Week

With the speed of a tortoise
And the drive of a sloth
I barrel towards infinity

A book in one hand
Coffee in the other
We phase through each other
Passing and passing
Until we're jumbled up together
Tossed like a salad
And mushed into some amorphous blob
Of caffeine and sentence structures
And whatever I add to the mix

This gooey blob of responsibility continues
On its ever important trek
Slowly crawling at such breakneck speeds

Peter Michalski
Poemod 61

Time To Feed

Do not settle pigs,

For the corn they throw your way.

Take the bread and run

Andrew Normington

Poemod 61

Quick Change

Jump into clothes

Then out

Then in again

Leave them for what they are

Only temporary flames

To be cast aside to whoever's in the wings

But make it quick

This train stops for no one

Peter Michalski

Poemod 62

A Hand Was Lent

Plunged beneath the surface,

Drowning in dirt and loneliness,

The carcass fends for itself.

Shielded from reality with cheap boards,

Olive planks soon to rot away,

Darkness sifts in through the cracks.

The flesh was overcome,

The coffin dissolved with time

There is nothing but dust—

The remains of human effort.

Each corpse secretes nutrients,

Leaking life for organisms,

Strengthening the decomposition.

Filled with bodies,

The underneath supplies itself,

Every burial is final.

Till those voices from above,

Pulse the veins of the fallen;

Turning olive planks to paper,

With commandment and psalm.

Each voice becomes clearer,

Bringing dust to breath,

The darkness is dug from the grave.

Those single hands rip away coffins,

Brutalized by scourging and splinters,

Never forgetting the mission.

Andrew Normington

Poemod 62

A Shameful Haiku

It's really a shame
Writing quick haikus because
Poetry takes time

Peter Michalski

Poemod 63

Helmet

The skull is cracked

When cats purr on millions

The blood leaks in.

Drops at a time—

the life fades away,

No one can see

the poison on the inside.

Though everyone sees the collision.

Crowds cheer

As I sleep here insane

Dazed in a memory of glory

Now I cannot think clearly

Except of those days

When I wish my head were safer

So I could wake up

Then think normally,

But I am sleeping here

Better off dead.

Andrew Normington

Poemod 63

Yet Another Shameful Haiku

Haikus aren't for me

The poems of yesteryear

Are pissing me off

Peter Michalski

Poemod 64

Minds Collide

Those days were growing
From their longest to their shortest
As the air went cold
And light dimmed with winter.

So too my memories faded;
Broken with each tackle.
I could not recall the faces
Of my nearest companions.

All I could remember,
When my sanity collapsed,
Were the cheering crowds
That brought lights to my fame.

The coaches told me:
My skull could take it—
The brutality of a man's game
While their pockets overflowed.

I am not able now
To heal the injuries.
And so I dissolve;
My helmet has failed me.

These days are growing
From their shortest to their last
As the air stops pumping
And my mind dims from reality.

Andrew Normington
Poemod 64

Applause High

It melts into your ears—

The warmth filling your head

And energizing your body

It shakes you, urges you

To dance

To sing

To exist as another

It gives you a strength unseen before

A steroid without the mess

Coursing and pulsing

Through every vein, artery, and crevice within

Building you into a massive force

A toned blob of joy and excitement

Unstoppable by all

Peter Michalski

Poemod 65

133

Morning After

Haiku Haiku Hai
What a stupid way to live
Hia hia hi

Andrew Normington
Poemod 65

Necessary Evil

Let my poems be omelets

To the eggs of the books I destroy

I pray for some reason

For the sacrifice of so many trees

Soldiers hacked to death

So that I may create something

Is it worth it?

Peter Michalski

Poemod 66

Reunion

Those dancing feet,

Keep me longing for the street.

Still the night is young

And I must remember where I am.

Not everything is Broadway,

But most everything is amazing.

If you take the time to look around

You might just be glad

To reunite

With those friends you lost in winter.

Andrew Normington

Poemod 66

Surround Yourself

They say surround yourself with those you admire

So I find myself in a sparkly green vest

Singing and dancing in ways I never thought possible

And those I admire

Those superstars, leagues above me

Those kings and queens who rule their lands

As I live in peasantry

They join me

And no one is anyone anymore

We sing and dance as one

Peter Michalski

Poemod 67

Missed The Game

What my heart has deemed acceptable,

Rejects the values of my mind.

There is no truth

To what they were doing

There is no hope to find.

The innocence is plagued

As the mind blurs

And the tongue is hot with liquor.

I am tortured by those flames.

Not mine, but her's

Her decisions

Before the game.

I was never at the game

Still I longed to be there.

I would not have been happy with what I saw.

Her hellish light

Burned bright with alcohol

Thank God, I was asleep.

Thank God I missed the game.

Andrew Normington

Poemod 67

See

Slink into a seat

See to it

That no one sees you

Because you see,

What it means to be seen

Is to die.

Peter Michalski

Poemod 68

Predictable

Life is math.

Every molecule knows where it's going

And we would too

If we knew the math

And had the time.

Everything that happens

Was going to happen

Since the beginning of time.

So while you predict your end

Do not forget

The emotions

You never saw coming.

Andrew Normington

Poemod 68

Clocks

Without a clock, how can one know?

Where they're to be

Or how

Or why

Take the dinosaurs

A prime example

They had no clocks

And now they are to fuel cars

I, for one, have no desire

To slosh about in some clunker

No siree

So clocks I carry

On arm and pocket they make their homes

And it must be two

For just one could be dishonest

And force me to implode

In a gas tank

Peter Michalski

Poemod 69

Tricky Tricky

Insanity is a common trick

Played from fool to fool

To suggest a way of living

Separated from the rules.

This place is bred from nights awake

Working or thinking—

Never both

And until you laugh away

The third joke too far

You will never realize

Just how insane you are.

Andrew Normington

Poemod 69

Squirrel

Give and take and jump around a bit

Between shrubs and hedges

Fly across power lines

Superhighways minus the gas

But be sure to jump

Never step

Peter Michalski

Poemod 70

Ball Game

Welcome to humanity,

We love our balls.

Big balls,

Small balls,

Bouncy balls,

Baseballs.

All balls bring entertainment

Man

Balls are great.

Andrew Normington

Poemod 70

We Will Fight On The Beaches

Behold, the shoreline's magnificence

A border, a bucket, to keep the land contained

A gateway to blue oblivions

That wears down the earth in steady erosion

A handful of sand

Infinitesimal amongst the string of grain

Takes its post

Joins its battalion

To fight the two sided war

To keep a peace between solid and liquid

To justify its own existence

The handful weeps

For it knows its place

Peter Michalski

Poemod 71

Frat Bros

The frattiest of frat cats
Lounge on their lawn chairs
Judging their prospects:
The female.
The greek interpretations
Fall short or necessary
Or accurate.
The memories of all
Are remembered with beer
So that all can be merry
And make memories forever.

Andrew Normington
Poemod 71

Grounded

Bask in a blue light

As the world continues without you

As revels abandon you on the roadside

As your bedroom welcomes you with a pitiful arm

Because you aren't that cunning

Peter Michalski

Poemod 72

College

Life's pretty dull

Just wait

Keep hoping

For those college days

When everything changes

Andrew Normington

Poemod 72

Panic

To be fine is a blessing.

Don't take it for granted.

Why must a knee be thrown into my chest

To steal the wind from my lungs

Why must there be chains

To lock me in place

And why must tendrils slither up my wet legs

And into my nose, ears, mouth

And grow and expand and engorge

And fill me in ways I hate beyond belief

And slither back out, leaving me shaking

To attack.

The Lord revoked his blessing.

Peter Michalski

Poemod 73

Leaky Faucet

drip drop

Slippery slop

The hand falls

To where it should not.

Of course it was coming;

Earth has its prophets.

Though thinking back on it

It's not a big deal.

What else is there anyway.

Andrew Normington

Poemod 73

Midnight

Quite late or early?
I guess that just depends on
When you're waking up

Peter Michalski

Poemod 74

Closing In

Orphan, orphaned

Child, forgotten.

Picked up by the only mother

The only one who cared.

That precious mother

Staring down at perfection.

Cradling and nurturing

Out of the purest

Virgin love.

Each child has a mother

Given by the Son.

You will always be an infant

Swaddled in her arms.

The emeralds in her crown

Twinkle like stars for the baby.

And the eyes too,

As perfect and green.

Glow as a child of Mary,

Perfect in the eyes of God.

Andrew Normington

Poemod 74

Time's Monarchy

Let kings and queens be banished from their thrones

Their usurper reigns, and will from now on

He takes firm grasp of his subjects

Withers them slowly

Becomes the sun to their grape

Leaving raisins behind

He impeaches interests from their minds

Preferring slavery instead

For it's much more efficient

And he orders a march

Forever

In his name

Peter Michalski

Poemod 75

Awww, Snap! Awww, Snap!

As the warmth of summer air swells into my moist armpits

And the strands of blonde glory dangle from my chin

Perhaps there is a chance for time.

A time where poems can squirt from the mind of idle adolescents

A time where young blondes work the isles

Falling in love

Probably not

And Rome gangs puzzle late into the night

Maybe even a pool party

If those still exist

Alas there is still work to do

Money to be made

So next year's adventures can be accounted for

But now I'll pretend to think

That school's end

Brings me time

For macaroni parties

And taking a nap.

Andrew Normington

Poemod 75

We would like to thank our families, our friends, and our high school English department for their contributions to Poemod. Without all the love, support, guidance, and inspiration these wonderful people provided, this book would surely not exist, and more importantly, we would not be the people we are today.

Thank you.

-Peter Michalski and Andrew Normington